Read My Lips
An Intimate, Sapphic Acrostic Poetry Collection

Dani Wilde

TEHOM
CENTER

Tehom Center Publishing is a 501(c)3 nonprofit publishing feminist and queer authors, with a commitment to elevate BIPOC writers. Its face and voice is Rev. Dr. Angela Yarber.

Paperback ISBN: 978-1-966655-27-5

Ebook ISBN: 978-1-966655-33-6

Contents

for her
for me
for you

Introduction

I wrote my first love poem in sixth grade. It was for a boy who most of my friends had a crush on whose name I haven't thought of in years, though I recall with perfect clarity how I struggled over each line, desperate to capture something I didn't actually feel. The words felt borrowed from mixtapes and movies meant to teach girls like me what love *should* look like.

Decades later, I'm still writing poems…but now they spill from a place of truth so raw it sometimes frightens me.

These poems explore intimacy in all its forms: the physical elation of what it feels like to touch and be touched by a woman; the emotional yearning to love and be loved; and the spiritual connections that tether us to our sapphic ancestors and to the cosmos. But they are also about the trust and intimacy we nurture with ourselves—the slow and sometimes painful process of unlearning shame and embracing desire as sacred and liberating.

My first ever published collection, this is also a love letter to my own mind, body, and soul. I have perhaps never been more open in my queerness than in these pieces, and there is a visceral weight lifted having expressed what has long been suppressed. It's an intentionally explicit resistance to the silencing of queer love, centering instead queer desire and sexual agency as acts of radical visibility. Especially now.

I grew up in a religious household, hearing what many LGBTQ+ people do: to be gay is sinful, and sinners go to hell. My child self interpreted that as, "Well I can't possibly be gay because *I am good!*" (I wish I could go back and bear hug her.) So I conformed to what the world expected from me, stuffing my sexuality into the bottom of a box it would take me until my early twenties to dust off.

Coming out in early adulthood—*finally* stepping into my queerness— might've been the first time I truly saw myself (*Oh! There she is.*). And I've spent every day since getting to know and love her more deeply. What a revelation to discover that the burning I felt was not damnation but the flame of my own becoming. My own power. Ferociously flowing from my fingertips, onto these pages.

Read My Lips is an invitation and a reclamation. These words are mine, but they belong to you—and to anyone who has ever looked in the mirror and struggled to recognize themselves, who has ever felt the terror of speaking their truth, who has ever loved so deeply that language itself seemed insufficient to contain it.

When I began writing, I didn't set out to create acrostics; the form found me. Each vertical word became an invocation to embody the essence of the word it spells. There is something deeply satisfying to me about hiding meaning in plain sight—perhaps because I spent so many years doing the same with my identity. Being queer often involves learning to read between the lines, to dig deep for meaning through obstacles, to find yourself in the margins of stories not written for you.

One of my early readers said something that stuck with me: *"You were successful in making me feel like both the speaker and the subject of each poem. I can feel how much you love, admire, and regard women. I can feel the journey of self love you've gone on and how you want every woman to love herself too."*

That's exactly what I hope this collection offers you: permission to see and love yourself—and others—more fully.

Thank you for picking up this book. For exploring intimacy. For resisting those who may never know love like we do. For daring to feel it all.

Read my lips: You are *loved*. You *are* love.

With desire and defiance,
Dani

Proceed with Caution

These poems are intimate and sexually explicit in nature.
You may want to read in a place without prying eyes.

Hunger

How I long to devour you, the way I've been
Unfed; I've prayed for this prey, starving for
Nourishment...salivating at the thought of
Gulping you like sweet, warm honey—
Every taste somehow leaves me craving more,
Ravenous to swallow the next mouthful.

Ache

Anticipation building as I
Clench around nothing, envisioning
How you'll treasure me—*finally*—
Edging me to ecstasy.

Desire

Delirious with want, the
Embers inside of me ignite from a simmer into a
Searing *need*…
Incinerating what I thought want even was;
Rekindled—stronger—with each breath of oxygen,
Engulfing me in your warmth.

Cuddle

Curl up next to me,
Undressed and sated…
Drawing my fingers
Down your spine,
Limbs loosening as we drift
Easily off to sleep.

Whisper

Would you like to
Hear a secret?
I'm desperate to make you come undone. Here. Now.
Shh, we have to keep quiet—
Purr vibrating against my palm; my
Ears collect your muzzled moans—
Rendering me speechless.

Beg

Body shaking,
Euphoria leaking from your lips, pleading for release like the
Good girl you are.

Fingers

Feverish to feel you, whether
Intertwined with your hands,
Nestled inside of you,
Gripping the silky strands of your hair,
Embraced by the moisture of that mouth,
Roaming to explore what's been untouched, or
Splayed across your chest, counting your heartbeats.

Satin

Smooth and shiny, you fasten knots
Around my wrists, then fashion a blindfold—
Tempering my gifts of touch and sight,
Intensifying every sensation…shaking, tugging, squeezing—
Notching both bedposts, until I let go.

Lips

Lingering one moment longer, the hot air swallows the
Inches between us, mouths
Parting just enough to inhale the space where restraint used to be.
Smiling before giving in to the tingling…closer, closer.

Thirst

Tongue lapping every drop, your
Heat leaves me parched,
Intoxicated by drinking you in like
Red wine—the decadence of each full-bodied
Sip as it hits my lips…unquenched,
Tipping my chin back to drain you.

Pegada

Pull me closer so I can be
Entangled in you, limb to limb as you
Guide me forward,
Anticipating your every move, as we
Dance like our souls have been
Attuned across lifetimes.

Intimacy

I'll show you mine if you show me yours—
Naked from the inside out.
Touch me in ways others can't. Or won't.
Is this what you wanted? To
Make love to my mind, to
Adventure into my heart, to
Cherish my soul, to fulfill my
Yearning to be truly seen? To be known?

Stay

Sleep here tonight because
Touching you is not enough—I need my
Arms blanketed around you so
You can dream about us.

Kiss Me

Knots twisting low in my stomach
Imagining the warmth of your lips—
Salivating as I shut my eyes and lean in…
Softness stealing my breath; our tongues tell the story of your
Mouth on mine, swallowing your satisfied sighs…
Encased by the taste of you.

Moan

Muffled whimpers undulate into
Octaves as your
Arousal amplifies—my
Name a chorus on your lips.

Strap On

Silicon tip swirling, coating me with you, before I slip inside.
Thrusting—further, faster—
Riding the waves of your hips,
Anchoring you in pleasure,
Pumping, penetrating deeper, before you suck
Off your sweet
Nectar.

Sit On My Face

Straddle my skull and smother me.
I can't think of a better way to die than to be
Trapped between your thighs while you're
On your knees,
Needy for release. Yes, love…
Move those hips,
Yank my hair,
Fuck my mouth,
Arch that back as you
Clench and come around my tongue—
Evidence you'll soon clean up.

Goddess

Getting on my knees to worship at the altar
Of her: Praying to the holiness of her lips;
Dancing to the hymn of her hips;
Devoted to the divinity of her mind and the
Eucharist between her thighs…Yes, I've tasted
Salvation, and it's the flavor of her—her
Spirit is my scripture; her body my bible.

Blush

Beneath my gaze, that pink hue blooms and
Lathers atop your cheeks—the
Undeniable color of wanting, a
Shy confession of
How you fantasize about me.

Darling

Delicate but not fragile—
A single word
Reserved only for her yet a
Language all its own. An
Ineffable endearment—
Novelizing the fated
Graduation from friends to lovers.

Hips

Hypnotizing me with your
Irresistible curves, it's a
Primal poetry how you
Sway with sovereignty.

Wet

Waves of pleasure
Endlessly washing over me as you
Trickle down my chin.

Strip

Stalking you with my eyes as you
Tantalize me…
Removing my resolve alongside each
Item of clothing, stealing my
Patience—a prisoner to the perfection of you.

Bed

Bones braided, it's a blessing to end the day
Enveloped beneath your sheets,
Disheveled and dreaming of you.

Phone Sex

Press dial when you need to
Hear my voice while you're
Overseas, deprived of me.
Narrate your every move…
Expect to spare no detail as you
Switch on your vibrator, parting both lips—
Electricity humming between us, a live wire,
X-rated preview of what's waiting when I finally make my way to you.

Taste

Tongue tingling at your
Aroma before licking you,
Savoring the flavor of you—
Tangy and sweet like summer fruit,
Edacious appetite to feast on your flesh.

Orgasm

Open your legs so I can
Run my tongue along your
Gorgeous cunt.
Abandon your careful control and
Silence your active mind—
Melting as they multiply.

Worthy

Wars I've won, fighting
On the side of self-love; I will not
Retreat when it comes to the
Truth of what I deserve—
Healing the patterns that harmed me,
Yielding to nothing less than everything.

Lingerie

Lace accentuates every
Intriguing inch of you, playing a
Naughty game of hide and seek,
Gifted in ribbons and straps I intend to unwrap—
Enticing me to
Rip it off with my teeth and
Indulge in what's underneath…
Exquisite torture.

Curves

Crafted by a sculptor, your
Unbridled silhouette defies straight lines,
Rebelling against rigidity.
Voluptuous—a masterpiece in motion,
Engraving itself beneath my hands as they trace the
Sacred shape of you.

Fuck Me

Feral and tightly wound, I need you to
Unravel me—dissipate my defenses.
Circle me slowly then sink inside.
Knuckles buried deep, you
Make a glorious mess of me…
Emptying me entirely.

Eye Contact

Eagerness from across the room,
Your gaze pins me in place, holding an
Entire conversation without a single word—
Chemistry binding strangers, friction pulling me forward…
Orbiting the room to find the quickest route to you.
Noise dimming as I draw nearer, seeing you clearer.
Triangulating from lashes to lips—
Affirming what we already know…
Can you see how my pupils dilate as I
Think about taking you home tonight?

Submission

Surrender isn't weakness; it's knowing who to bend for.
Under my command, you'll find freedom.
Bound by trust, not by force.
My voice is a tether,
Idling your body between desire and discipline—
Sweet girl, just do what I
Say, and I won't make you beg.
Incessant patience will be rewarded.
Observe, listen, and obey...
Now get on your hands and knees and wait.

Dominate

Discipline is an art, and I paint you in restraint.
Observing the details of how
My power can protect you,
Instructing your movements—
Navigating throughout punishment and pleasure.
Abdicate your authority,
Test the limits of your tolerance, with an
Explicit, enthusiastic *yes*.

Choke

Constrict my circulation,
Hands pressing firmly, launching me into
Outer space—a galaxy without gravity.
Knowing exactly when to release my throat—
Exhaling as I return to earth.

Flirt

Forget tomorrow—
Let's have some fun being
Infatuated with the idea of one another; I can't
Resist your charm…
Teased by the game we both play to lose.

Pulse

Pierce my earlobe between your teeth, throbbing
Under the skin of my neck—pooling, melting
Lower…lower…and lower still.
Stomach surging and coiling, heartbeat
Escalating where I crave you most.

Masturbate

My imagination drifts to you
After a lonely day…
Settling back into my pillow,
Tantalizing myself,
Undulating my stress,
Relief buzzing,
Biting my lip as I work harder
Against my own hand—
Tightening, trembling…
Echoing your name.

Sapphic

Seduced by every
Angle of her collarbones and convictions, she's a
Priestess—a poetess—both myth and mortal,
Potent and prolific as the Tenth Muse herself—
Her heart, an open portal to Lesbos,
Inscribed on papyrus scrolls, consecrating the
Covenant of women who've dared to desire.

Smile

Smirking like you're
Making love to the world—
Inviting me into joy with the
Laughter spilling from your lips,
Ethereal in the way it lingers as we kiss.

Pussy

Plump and pulsing, you
Urge me to unbutton your jeans and
Submerge my fingers into your heat—
Soaked and succulent,
Your heady perfume smells good enough to eat.

Pleasure

Pouring passion into you, patiently.
Listening and learning the architecture of your body,
Easing closer to the blueprint of bliss—adorned with
Artwork framed in the arch of your back,
Scaffolding built by your screams,
Unlocking the door with the master key I own, to a
Room I want to reside in—your
Essence surrounding me for eternity.

Yearning

Yesterday I was whole, but today I
Exist in fragments—a ghost of what I was…
Aching for your affection,
Remembering touching you in ways I haven't,
Numbing the beaming hope you awakened,
Imprisoned by the words I cannot say,
Nostalgic for the risk of falling for you, fully…
Guarded—still I wait for you anyway.

Dirty Talk

Darling, you make me so fucking wet.
I want you so full of me you forget your own name.
Remember who you belong to—every inch of you is *mine*.
That's it…Eyes on me…Breathe with me.
You can handle more. Do you want more?
There you go…Fuck. *Just* like that.
Ask nicely, and maybe I'll give you what you want.
Listen to me…Not until I say so. Do you understand?
Keep going…Stay with me…Good girl. Now come for me.

Rough

Rip open my clothes.
Overwhelmed by your intensity,
Untamed—a wildfire ravaging me whole,
Generously branding my skin,
High from the scarlet wreckage.

Hands

Hugging my jaw,
Anchoring me in the moment,
Nails massaging declarations down my spine,
Dexterous in their ability to hold me—
Steady. Deliberate. Certain.

Muse

Magnetic, your energy attracts me in—an
Uncontained, ultraviolet glow. My
Soul recognizes and co-creates with yours…an
Enigmatic, magnificent force of nature.

Good Girl

Greedy for praise; eager to please.
Oh, it's so sexy how your body listens better than you do—
Occupying the subconscious corners of your mind,
Disobedient yet desperate for attention. Follow my
Gentle guidance, or my detailed demands.
Intuitively, I know what you need—and you don't know the
Reverence you show when you
Let me teach you a lesson.

Sweat

Slick skin glistening from
Working you toward the finish line,
Endurance strengthening alongside my
Addiction to your pheromones…
Torso tense, muscles drenched as I demolish you.

Scissor

Spreading against one another, the
Conductor our clits…
Instrument strings tuned impossibly tight,
Sensual percussion of pressure,
Symphony of our moist music carefully
Orchestrated—
Rhythmic. Raw. Resolution.

Tattoos

Twitching to trace what
Accentuates—contour of colors and inked
Tales from chapters preceding mine,
Toughened against the world but tender to my touch.
Ornate with memories and messages…
Outlined in hope, in hurt, in healing—scanning the
Story of you, fingering through every page.

Lust

Limerence or love: do you know the difference?
Unrequited. You must choose to
Succumb to insanity or serenity—infatuated by the
Thrill of the chase, but tension eventually breaks.

Fantasy

Forbidden boundaries I only dare cross in dreams,
Abandoning reality for worlds behind my eyelids.
Nighttime becomes a sanctuary for my secrets,
Tempted by my unconscious creations.
Afraid of waking…
Sleeping just a little longer—
Yesterday was the last time I didn't search for you in daylight.

Woman

Wild or tame, we carry multitudes—
Orchestrations of the divine feminine,
Mad with magic,
Alchemists of empathy and ferocity,
Nurturers of love and life itself.

Love

Longevity. What an honor to
Observe your life unfold, to witness the
Vibrant iterations of your soul—
Expanding, then transmuting timelines when the end inevitably arrives.

Nipples

Nestled near your heart,
I burrow between the
Peaks that feed—one hand
Pinching and palming, the other
Licking and lavishing, bottling
Excitement like a champagne cork ready to burst—
Shaken breaths intensify your heaving chest.

Erotic

Explosions that cannot be extinguished.
Ravaging my neck with your intensity,
Obstructing my escape—destruction in your wake…
Temperature rising as you descend, each degree emits the
Immeasurable ways I want you—
Consuming me as I burn for you.

Naked

Name every scar, and I won't flinch—
Adoring the shield you drop at your feet,
Knowing air is the single barrier existing between us…
Exposing the layers you've learned to protect.
Don't you dare rush to cover up—let me *see* you.

Fate

Future meets past, a force without mass, yet still I manifest you
Across dimensions—our love
Transcends time and folds space in half—
Entropy, or divine entanglement?

Hair

Haloing your beautiful face before I
Affix it in my fist—cascading curtains roped back,
Interwoven between my fingers,
Reining you in at the nape of your willing neck.

Pillow

Precious of your perfume to spend the night though you didn't,
Imprinting your impermanence—
Languishing for love that wakes and stays, unburdened by the
Light of morning while the coffee brews,
Oneiric stillness between our bones—
Wrapping, instead, the loose stitch around my finger.

Naughty

Normalcy may bore, so we
Augment reality when we step outside the door—
Underwear packing an undetectable game,
Gauging how much you can take before the facade breaks;
Helpless to when I click the power on, pacing you toward the precipice,
Tying a tourniquet with your legs to thwart the thrill of being caught,
Yelling with your eyes: stop *right* now; *please* don't stop.

Buttocks

Bruised red under the weight of my hands,
Ushering the movements of that
Thick throne—
Take your seat.
Open palms cupping my ankles,
Cushions rippling as you buck backward,
Kneading your waist while *needing*—
Stupefied by how you ride me in reverse.

Sexy

Shoulders back. Chin up. Command the space you
Earned—the epitome of confidence, extending a
Xenial invitation to fill rooms once empty and dimly lit…
You radiate ambition, holding the door open behind you.

Shower

Steaming water rains down,
Healing an honest week's work,
Overflowing devotion drips from your fingertips—
Wholesome, you rinse away my hurt,
Exfoliating until the ache evaporates,
Renewed for tomorrow—a clean slate.

Pride

Promise me this: you will
Resist, for we are
Infinite in our capacity to love,
Decorating history with bricks—
Effervescent, our existence endures.

Read My Lips

Reclaiming my time, for I am not a woman who will
Evaporate into nothingness; I will live to feel
Alive, to speak my truth, to silence my shame—
Daring to leave behind, with forgiveness and gratitude, the woman I once was,

Moving toward the woman I am and the woman I have
Yet to awaken—slumbering though stirring beneath the surface.

Listen: my spirit remembers what they once taught my mind to suppress.
I vow to never forget to love myself—so I will be unapologetic in
Pursuing the intimacy I desire and deserve:
Spiritual. Mental. Emotional. Physical. Cosmic. Hers. Mine.

Acknowledgments

To my found queer family whose love, support, confidence, humor, resilience, compassion, and vulnerability made me feel safe enough to grow into and express a more empowered version of myself:

Adri, Angelica A., Angelica B., Angelica CK, Betsy, Caroline, Chris, Dani, Di (especially for the name of this collection!), Fiona, Flavia, JoJo, Kayla, Monique, Vivi, and Willow.

I love you all.

About the Author

Dani Wilde is a queer, multi-passionate millennial and feeler of too many things. She writes to alchemize ache into art, and her work explores identity, grief, intimacy, and hope. Her debut collection, *Read My Lips*, explores sapphic intimacy through acrostic poetry. After years of pretending to be a normal adult in corporate jobs, she now runs her own business—answering the call of creativity and self-expression that long lived in the notes app of her phone. She is passionate about building community and squeezing the juice out of life. When not writing, she's probably somewhere overthinking everything while reading a good book in dog-hair-covered sweatpants.